MARVELOUS
Chicken
RECIPES

KÖNEMANN

❖ MARVELOUS CHICKEN RECIPES ❖

Choosing your chicken

Chicken is a versatile and affordable food that is eaten all over the world. It is a complete protein, with minerals such as potassium and phosphorus, as well as some B vitamins, and without its skin, it is relatively low in fat.

Buying chicken

Fresh and frozen
If buying fresh chicken, take it out of its packaging and store on a plate, loosely covered with waxed paper. Remove any giblets from the cavity and store separately. If you're not using it right away, place in the coldest part of the refrigerator, taking care not to store it on a shelf above any cooked food. The chicken should be kept cold at all times, including while you are traveling home from shopping. The chicken can also be frozen for up to 3 months by sealing it in a freezer bag with the air expelled (make sure you write the date on a label). Defrost chicken carefully as bacteria, such as salmonella, can be activated if it gets too warm. Defrost in the fridge, not under running water or at room temperature. If you are defrosting in a microwave, stick to chicken pieces because whole chickens defrost unevenly. Place the chicken so that the larger part of each piece is facing outwards.

1 Preparing the chicken for the microwave.

Free-range and corn-fed
These chickens are now widely available. Free-range chickens can be identified by a label stating their place of origin and that they have been reared humanely. They have a better flavor and texture than intensively farmed chickens. Corn-fed chickens have a yellow skin and flesh, but are not necessarily free-range.

Cuts

Whole chicken
Traditionally whole chickens are roasted, but they are also delicious poached, barbecued, spit-roasted, boned and stuffed. The Broiler-fryer can weigh up to $3^{1}/_{2}$ pounds and will feed 4 people. As the name implies, it's best when broiled or fried. Roasters, weighing between $2^{1}/_{2}$ and 5 pounds, are more flavorful, with a high fat content, and roast beautifully. Depending on size, a roaster will feed 4 to 6.

To prepare a chicken for roasting, first make sure that there is nothing inside the cavity (the giblets and neck are sometimes stored in the cavity in a plastic bag). Trim off any excess fat with a pair of poultry shears, rinse inside the cavity, then pat dry the skin and cavity with a paper towel. Truss the chicken by tying the legs together, then tucking the wings behind the body.

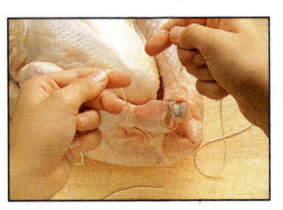

2 Trussing a whole chicken.

❖ CHOOSING YOUR CHICKEN ❖

The body cavity of the chicken can harbor bacteria, so if stuffing, be sure to cook the chicken right away and check that it is cooked through to the center of the stuffing. Chickens can also be successfully stuffed under the skin.

3 Stuffing the chicken under the skin.

Set the oven to 400°F and cook the chicken for 20 minutes per pound. Test by inserting a skewer into the thickest part of the thigh—if the juices run clear, the chicken is cooked. If the juices are pink, then cook for another 10 minutes, then re-test. The internal temperature of the bird should be 180°F. Rest the chicken, wrapped in foil, for 10 minutes before carving, to allow the juices to settle.

Breasts
Chicken breasts are available on the bone and also as skinless, boned breast halves with the tenderloin strip attached. Breasts are the whitest and largest portions of meat on the chicken. They can be roasted, steamed, fried, broiled or barbecued, as well as stuffed or wrapped. Be careful not to overcook as they can dry out.

Thigh-and-leg quarters
The thigh and drumstick in one piece is good for baking, barbecuing, breading and frying. Thigh quarters take some time to cook through to the bone and need to be tested with a skewer to make sure the juices are clear. All chicken on the bone should be slashed before cooking to make sure that it cooks right through.

Thighs
A thigh is a darker, more succulent meat than breast, and works well in curries and stews, and as kebabs and satays. Thighs are available on the bone as well as skinless, boned pieces.

4 Testing the chicken with a skewer.

Drumsticks
Chicken drumsticks are great as finger food and for barbecues. They are also good for children, and when cold can be served in lunchboxes or for picnics. Drumsticks should be slashed before cooking.

5 Slashing thighs and drumsticks.

Wings
Wings can be marinated and then broiled, barbecued or baked to make great finger food. They are also useful for making quick chicken stocks.

Ground chicken
Chicken flesh can be ground and used for anything that you would use ground beef or pork for. Try chicken burgers, lasagne, terrines and kebabs.

Livers
Chicken livers are a rich source of iron and are delicious as a pâté or pan-fried for salads. Cut off any greenish bits during preparation and make sure you clean the livers well.

❖ MARVELOUS CHICKEN RECIPES ❖

Brilliant chicken recipes

Chicken is the most versatile of foods—perfect for both an economical family dinner or a quick-and-easy meal for two.

❖ ❖ ❖

Chicken Caesar salad

Preparation time:
  20 minutes
Total cooking time:
  20 minutes
Serves 3–4

Dressing
1/3 cup olive oil
1–2 cloves garlic, crushed
2 tablespoons lemon juice
6 canned anchovies, chopped
1 egg yolk
1/4 cup whipping cream

1/2 day-old French baguette
oil, for deep-frying
3 skinless, boned chicken breast halves
1 tablespoon Dijon mustard
1 romaine lettuce, torn into pieces
1/4 cup Parmesan shavings

1. To make the dressing, combine all the ingredients together in a jar and shake well. Refrigerate.
2. Cut the bread into 1/2 inch cubes and deep-fry in batches until golden. Drain on paper towels to absorb any excess oil.
3. Preheat the broiler. Trim the chicken of any excess fat or sinew. Brush lightly with the mustard and sprinkle with some ground black pepper. Broil each side for 4–6 minutes, or until the chicken is cooked in the center. Cover and stand for a few minutes while preparing the salad.
4. Toss the lettuce, dressing and croutons together and place in a large serving dish. Slice the chicken breasts into 6–8 slices and arrange on top. Sprinkle with the Parmesan and serve while still warm.

NUTRITION PER SERVE (4)
Protein 35 g; Fat 45 g; Carbohydrate 25 g; Dietary Fiber 3 g; Cholesterol 130 mg; 625 calories

Chicken Caesar salad

❖ MARVELOUS CHICKEN RECIPES ❖

✧ Marvelous Chicken Recipes ✧

Lemon baked chicken

Preparation time:
  15 minutes
Total cooking time:
  1 3/4 hours
Serves 4

1 x 3 lb chicken
2 lemons, coarsely chopped
4 green onions, chopped
2 tablespoons chopped fresh lemon thyme
2 cloves garlic, crushed
1 tablespoon olive oil
6 sprigs fresh lemon thyme
4 thin slices prosciutto

1. Preheat the oven to 350°F. Trim the chicken of any excess fat, then rinse the cavity and pat dry with paper towels.
2. Place the lemons in a bowl and add the green onions, chopped lemon thyme, garlic and some pepper and mix to combine. Spoon the mixture into the cavity of the chicken.
3. Bend the chicken wings back and tuck them behind the body. Tie the drumsticks together using string. Place in a roasting pan on a rack, brush with the oil and top with the lemon thyme. Cover the breast with overlapping slices of prosciutto.
4. Cover the chicken with aluminum foil and bake for 1 1/2 hours, or until cooked through. Remove the foil and cook for another 15 minutes, then allow the chicken to rest in a warm place for 15 minutes before carving. Discard the stuffing before serving.

NUTRITION PER SERVE
Protein 65 g; Fat 45 g; Carbohydrate 4.5 g; Dietary Fiber 2 g; Cholesterol 215 mg; 675 calories

Stir-fried sesame chicken and leek

Preparation time:
  15 minutes
Total cooking time:
  15 minutes
Serves 4–6

2 tablespoons sesame seeds
1 tablespoon oil
2 teaspoons sesame oil
1 lb 10 oz skinless, boned chicken breast halves, cut into thin diagonal strips
1 leek, white part only, julienned
2 cloves garlic, crushed
2 tablespoons soy sauce
1 tablespoon mirin or dry sherry
1 teaspoon sugar

1. Heat the wok until very hot, add the sesame seeds and dry-fry over high heat until they are golden. Remove the seeds from the wok.
2. Reheat the wok, add the oils and swirl them around to coat the sides. Stir-fry the chicken strips in 3 batches over high heat, tossing constantly, until they are just cooked. (Reheat the wok before cooking each batch of chicken.)
3. Return all the chicken to the wok, then add the julienned leek and garlic and cook for 2–3 minutes, or until the leek is soft and golden. Check that the chicken is cooked through; if it is not, cover the pan, reduce the heat and cook for another 2 minutes, or until it is cooked.
4. Add the soy sauce, mirin or sherry, sugar and the toasted sesame seeds to the pan and toss well to coat the chicken. Season with salt and freshly ground black pepper and serve the stir-fry immediately.

NUTRITION PER SERVE (6)
Protein 35 g; Fat 35 g; Carbohydrate 8 g; Dietary Fiber 0 g; Cholesterol 160 mg; 530 calories

Lemon baked chicken (top) with Stir-fried sesame chicken and leek

❖ Marvelous Chicken Recipes ❖

Chicken laksa

Preparation time:
25 minutes
Total cooking time:
20 minutes
Serves 4

1 tablespoon oil
2–3 tablespoons ready-made red curry paste
2 cups unsweetened coconut milk
3 cups chicken stock
1 lb 4 oz skinless, boned chicken thighs, cut into bite-size pieces
8 oz dried rice vermicelli noodles
8 deep-fried bean curd, halved on the diagonal
1 1/3 cups bean sprouts
1 short, thin cucumber, cut into short, thin strips
4 oz firm tofu, sliced into 8 pieces
1 tablespoon chili jam (chili paste in soy bean oil), optional
1/4 cup fresh mint leaves

1. Heat the oil in a wok or heavy-based skillet. Cook the paste over medium heat for 2–3 minutes or until fragrant. Add the coconut milk, stock and chicken, bring to a boil, then reduce the heat and simmer for 15 minutes, or until the chicken is cooked.
2. Bring a large saucepan of water to a boil. Add the noodles and cook until tender. Drain and divide among 4 deep bowls. Divide the deep-fried bean curd and half the bean sprouts into each bowl and ladle in the soup.
3. Garnish with the remaining sprouts, cucumber, tofu, chili jam and mint leaves. Serve with lime wedges.

NUTRITION PER SERVE
Protein 45 g; Fat 45 g; Carbohydrate 55 g; Dietary Fiber 1.5 g; Cholesterol 75 mg; 785 calories

Coconut chicken

Preparation time:
10 minutes
Total cooking time:
55 minutes
Serves 4

1/3 cup seasoned flour
4 chicken breast halves (with bone and skin on)
2 tablespoons oil
1 onion, chopped
1 small chile, finely chopped, optional
1 cup unsweetened coconut cream
1/4 cup mango chutney
pinch of ground turmeric
2 tablespoons chopped cilantro
1 tablespoon finely shredded lime rind (see Note)
2 tablespoons lime juice

1. Preheat the oven to 350°F. Place the seasoned flour on a sheet of waxed paper and toss the chicken in the flour until well coated, shaking off any excess. Heat the oil in a large heavy-based skillet and fry the chicken, in batches, until browned on all sides. Transfer to a shallow casserole dish.
2. Add the chopped onion and chile to the skillet and cook over medium heat until soft. Stir in the coconut cream, mango chutney and just enough ground turmeric to make the sauce a light golden color. Remove the pan from the heat, then slowly stir in the cilantro, lime rind and lime juice.
3. Pour the sauce over the chicken breasts in the casserole dish. Cover and bake, basting occasionally, for about 35 minutes, or until the chicken is tender and cooked through. Serve with steamed rice.

NUTRITION PER SERVE
Protein 40 g; Fat 40 g; Carbohydrate 15 g; Dietary Fiber 2 g; Cholesterol 150 mg; 450 calories

Note: Use a zester to shred the lime rind, or grate the rind on the fine side of a cheese grater.

Chicken laksa (top) with Coconut chicken

❖ Marvelous Chicken Recipes ❖

Chicken and mushroom pillows

Preparation time:
  40 minutes +
  30 minutes cooling.
Total cooking time:
  40 minutes.
Serves 4

10 oz skinless, boned chicken breast halves
1/4 cup butter
1 onion, finely chopped
1 clove garlic, chopped
5 oz *mushrooms, thinly sliced*
1 tablespoon green peppercorns, drained and coarsely chopped
1/4 cup all-purpose flour
1/2 cup whipping cream
1/2 cup milk
1 tablespoon chopped fresh parsley
6 sheets *phyllo pastry*
olive oil, for brushing
1/2 cup fresh, soft bread crumbs

1. Trim the chicken of any excess fat or sinew and cut into small cubes. Melt half the butter in a heavy-based skillet. When foamy, add the onion, garlic and chicken and cook for 5 minutes. Add the mushrooms and peppercorns, cover and cook for 2 minutes, or until soft.
2. Add the remaining butter. When melted, add the flour and stir for 2 minutes. Remove the pan from the heat and gradually stir in the cream and milk. Return to the heat, add the parsley, salt and pepper and bring to a boil, stirring. Spread into a flat dish and allow to cool for 30 minutes.
3. Preheat the oven to 350°F. Cover the phyllo with a damp towel. Working with one sheet at a time, lightly brush with the olive oil, top with the next sheet, brush with more oil, then top with a third sheet. Repeat with the remaining phyllo.
4. Cut both stacks of phyllo in half. Pile a quarter of the filling into the center of each half and spread out a little. Fold the bottom of the pastry up over the filling, then bring the top down. Fold the sides in, brushing with water, and press to seal. Turn the pillows over and place on a greased baking sheet. Brush the tops with a little oil and cut 2 slashes in each one. Sprinkle the bread crumbs over the pillows with some salt.
5. Bake the pillows for 25 minutes, or until golden and crisp.

NUTRITION PER SERVE
Protein 25 g; Fat 30 g; Carbohydrate 40 g; Dietary Fiber 3 g; Cholesterol 115 mg; 510 calories

Chicken and mushroom pillows

1 Brush each layer of phyllo with some olive oil.

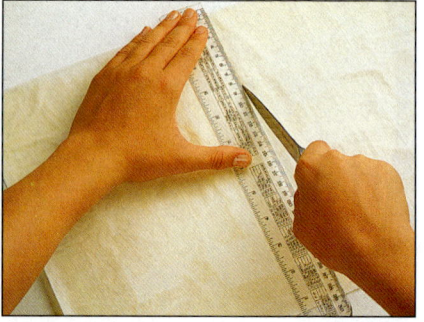

2 Cut the 2 stacks of layered phyllo pastry in half.

❖ **MARVELOUS CHICKEN RECIPES** ❖

3 Fold the bottom of the pastry up over the filling, then fold down the top.

4 Place the 4 pillows on a baking sheet, then brush with some oil and cut slashes.

11

Chicken pie

Preparation time:
  40 minutes + 30
  minutes chilling time
Total cooking time:
  50 minutes
Serves 6

*1/3 cup butter,
  chopped
2 oz cream cheese,
  chopped
2 cups all-purpose
  flour
2 eggs, lightly
  beaten
1/4 cup water
2 tablespoons oil
1 leek, chopped
2 cloves garlic,
  crushed
2 carrots, halved and
  sliced
1 stalk celery,
  chopped
1 cup frozen peas,
  thawed
1 3/4 cups chicken stock
2 tablespoons flour,
  extra
1 1/4 cups sour cream
1 large cooked chicken,
  skinned, boned and
  cut into long strips*

1. Preheat the oven to 400°F. Cut the butter and cream cheese into the flour until it resembles fine bread crumbs. Add half the egg and enough of the water to make the mixture cling together. Turn out onto a floured surface, gather the dough together and cover with plastic wrap. Chill for 30 minutes.
2. Heat the oil in a saucepan, add the leek and garlic and cook, stirring, for 5 minutes, or until the leek is soft. Add the carrots, celery, peas and 1 cup of the chicken stock and simmer for 5 minutes, or until the vegetables are tender. Blend the extra flour with the remaining stock and add to the pan. Stir until the mixture boils and thickens, then remove from the heat and add the sour cream; let cool. Add the chicken strips.
3. Cut the pastry in half and roll out one half on a lightly floured surface into a 12 inch round. Place on a lightly greased baking sheet. Spread the cooled filling over, leaving a 3/4 inch border. Roll the remaining pastry into a 13 inch round. Brush the border of the bottom pastry with the remaining egg, cover the filling with the second pastry round and press or twist the edges together to seal. Dust with flour and cut a small slit in the top.
4. Bake for 35–40 minutes, or until golden (cover loosely with foil if browning too much).

NUTRITION PER SERVE
Protein 55 g; Fat 60 g; Carbohydrate 40 g; Dietary Fiber 5 g; Cholesterol 265 mg; 915 calories

Apricot chicken

Preparation time:
  10 minutes
Total cooking time:
  55 minutes
Serves 4

*1 x 3 lb chicken, skin
  removed, cut into
  pieces
1 1/4 oz package French
  onion soup mix
2 cups canned apricot
  nectar
16 oz can apricot
  halves, drained*

1. Preheat the oven to 350°F. Place the chicken pieces in a casserole dish. Mix the French onion soup mix with the apricot nectar and pour over the chicken.
2. Bake, covered, for 50 minutes, then add the drained apricot halves and bake for another 5 minutes. Serve the chicken with creamy mashed potatoes or rice to soak up all the juices.

NUTRITION PER SERVE
Protein 30 g; Fat 3 g; Carbohydrate 25 g; Dietary Fiber 1.5 g; Cholesterol 60 mg; 250 calories

Chicken pie (top) with Apricot chicken

❖ **MARVELOUS CHICKEN RECIPES** ❖

❖ MARVELOUS CHICKEN RECIPES ❖

Chicken and corn chowder

Preparation time:
  15 minutes
Total cooking time:
  20 minutes
Makes 6 1/2 cups

1 tablespoon butter
5 green onions, finely chopped
2 slices bacon, finely chopped
1 stalk celery, finely chopped
1 lb potatoes, peeled and diced
2 cups chicken stock
1/2 cooked or barbecued chicken, diced
1 1/2 cups milk
14 oz can creamed corn
2 green onions, thinly sliced, to garnish

1. Melt the butter in a saucepan. Cook the green onions, bacon and celery over medium heat for 2–3 minutes, without coloring. Add the diced potatoes and cook for 1–2 minutes, then add the stock. Cook for 10 minutes, or until the potatoes are tender.
2. Add the chicken, milk and corn. Heat without boiling and stir frequently. Season with pepper and garnish with the green onions.

NUTRITION PER SERVE
Protein 45 g; Fat 30 g; Carbohydrate 40 g; Dietary Fiber 6 g; Cholesterol 140 mg; 140 calories

Chili barbecued chicken

Preparation time:
  30 minutes + 2–3 hours marinating
Total cooking time:
  1 hour
Serves 4

2 x 2 lb chickens
2 tablespoons olive oil

Barbecue sauce
1/4 cup olive oil
1/2 cup tomato ketchup
1 tablespoon red wine vinegar
2 cloves garlic, crushed
1 red onion, chopped
1 small red chile, seeded and chopped
1 small green chile, seeded and chopped
2 teaspoons mustard
2 teaspoons Worcestershire sauce
1 teaspoon dried oregano
pinch cayenne pepper
2 tablespoons lime juice
1–2 tablespoons sweet chili sauce

1. Using a pair of poultry shears, cut the chickens in half lengthwise along the breastbone and along each side of the backbone, discarding the backbone. Flatten gently, then thread onto metal skewers.
2. To make the barbecue sauce, place all the ingredients except the lime juice and chili sauce in a saucepan. Cook over low heat for 10 minutes. Cool, purée in a food processor, then add the juice and chili sauce.
3. Pour a third of the sauce into a bowl. Add the oil and brush thickly over the chickens, reserving some for basting. Cover and chill the chickens for 2–3 hours or overnight.
4. Preheat the oven to 350°F. Place the chickens on a rack in a roasting pan filled with enough water to cover its base. Brush with the marinade and bake for 40–50 minutes, or until cooked, basting frequently. Cut into quarters and serve with the remaining sauce.

NUTRITION PER SERVE
Protein 65 g; Fat 60 g; Carbohydrate 15 g; Dietary Fiber 2 g; Cholesterol 210 mg; 885 calories

Note: Increase the chile, cayenne and chili sauce for a more fiery flavor.

Chicken and corn chowder (top) with Chili barbecued chicken

Open sandwiches

Chicken is a great snack food, and these open sandwiches are perfect for an easy-to-make but stylish lunch. For super-quick open sandwiches, buy a barbecued chicken and just stack up the fillings.

Chicken and chargrilled vegetable sandwich

Chargrill 2 skinless, boned chicken breast halves. Cut into thin diagonal slices. Cut a Middle Eastern flat bread loaf into quarters. Brush lightly with olive oil mixed with a crushed garlic clove. Chargrill or broil until lightly browned. Spread with mayonnaise and arrange chargrilled vegetables such as eggplant, sweet bell peppers, zucchini and mushrooms on top. Finish with the chicken and some pesto. *Makes 4*

NUTRITION PER SERVE
Protein 25 g; Fat 10 g; Carbohydrate 35 g; Dietary Fiber 3.5 g; Cholesterol 40 mg; 330 calories

Chicken, asparagus and prosciutto sandwich

Chargrill 2 skinless, boned chicken breast halves, then cut into thin diagonal slices. Cut 4 slices from a sourdough loaf and brush lightly with olive oil mixed with a clove of crushed garlic. Chargrill or broil each side until lightly browned. Dry-fry 4 slices prosciutto and break into large pieces. Place 3–4 lightly cooked asparagus spears on each slice of bread and top with sliced plum tomatoes, the chicken slices, some watercress and a dollop of mayonnaise combined with some grainy mustard. Finish with the prosciutto. *Makes 4*

NUTRITION PER SERVE
Protein 15 g; Fat 10 g; Carbohydrate 30 g; Dietary Fiber 3 g; Cholesterol 25 mg; 280 calories

❖ OPEN SANDWICHES ❖

Crostini with chicken livers and broiled sweet peppers

Toast 8 slices French bread and keep warm. Cut 1 small red sweet bell pepper into quarters, seed and rub both sides with a tablespoon of oil. Broil both sides until soft, peel off the skin, then slice into thin slices. Clean 6 oz chicken livers, then cut into pieces. Fry a crushed clove garlic in a tablespoon of butter for 30 seconds, then add the chicken livers and sauté for 4–5 minutes (the livers should be just pink in the center). Remove. Add 2 tablespoons dry sherry and 1 teaspoon chopped fresh thyme to the pan and deglaze for 2 minutes over gentle heat. Season. Top the bread with the livers and spoon some juices over. Arrange the strips of pepper on top with a small sprig of thyme and freshly ground black pepper and salt. Serve warm. *Makes 8*

NUTRITION PER SERVE
Protein 15 g; Fat 10 g; Carbohydrate 12 g; Dietary Fiber 1.5 g; Cholesterol 35 mg; 210 calories

Chicken and avocado salsa sandwich

Chargrill 2 skinless, boned chicken breast halves, then cut into thin diagonal slices. Cut 4 thick slices from a crusty Italian loaf. Lightly toast or chargrill the bread. Make a salsa from 1 chopped avocado, 1 chopped peach or nectarine, 1 chopped tomato, 2 finely chopped green onions, 1 tablespoon chopped cilantro and 1–2 tablespoons lemon juice. Arrange romaine lettuce leaves, then chicken slices on the bread. Top each with the salsa and serve immediately. *Makes 4*

NUTRITION PER SERVE
Protein 15 g; Fat 9.5 g; Carbohydrate 30 g; Dietary Fiber 3 g; Cholesterol 20 mg; 280 calories

From left to right: Chicken and chargrilled vegetable sandwich; Chicken, asparagus and prosciutto sandwich; Crostini with chicken livers and broiled sweet peppers; Chicken and avocado salsa sandwich

❖ Marvelous Chicken Recipes ❖

Chicken bake

Preparation time:
 30 minutes
Total cooking time:
 1 hour 10 minutes
Serves 4

1 1/2 lb skinless, boned chicken thighs
2 tablespoons butter
1 onion, chopped
2 stalks celery, chopped
2 tablespoons flour
1 cup chicken stock
3/4 cup milk
4 oz cooked ham, thinly sliced
2 teaspoons coarse-grain mustard
2 tablespoons chopped fresh parsley
3 hard-cooked eggs, quartered
3 potatoes, peeled and very thinly sliced
1 tablespoon butter, melted
paprika, to garnish

1. Preheat the oven to 400°F. Trim the chicken thighs of any excess fat or sinew. Melt the butter in a skillet and cook the chicken in batches over high heat for 10 minutes, or until browned and cooked through. Remove from the pan. Add the chopped onion and celery and cook for 5 minutes until soft, then stir in the flour.
2. Remove from the heat and gradually add the stock and milk. Return to the heat and stir until the mixture boils and thickens. Cut the chicken into bite-size pieces and add to the pan with any juices, the ham, mustard and parsley; mix well and season. Stir in the eggs.
3. Spoon the mixture into a 6-cup capacity shallow baking dish. Layer the potatoes over the chicken, brush with the melted butter and sprinkle lightly with paprika.
4. Bake for 40–50 minutes until the potatoes are crisp and golden.

NUTRITION PER SERVE
Protein 55 g; Fat 20 g; Carbohydrate 20 g; Dietary Fiber 2.5 g; Cholesterol 295 mg; 505 calories

Chicken and mushroom sauté

Preparation time:
 15 minutes
Total cooking time:
 15 minutes
Serves 4

2 tablespoons olive oil
1 lb 4 oz skinless, boned chicken thighs, cut into bite-size chunks
2 tablespoons brandy
1/2 cup chicken stock
10 oz mushrooms, trimmed and thickly sliced
2 teaspoons fresh thyme leaves
1/4 cup whipping cream

1. Heat the oil in a heavy-based skillet until hot. Cook the chopped chicken, in batches, over a high heat for 4 minutes, or until browned all over. Reheat the pan in between batches. Remove the chicken and drain the oil from the pan.
2. Heat the pan until slightly smoking, pour in the brandy and allow it to bubble until it has nearly evaporated. Pour in the chicken stock and bring to a boil, then stir in the sliced mushrooms and thyme, and season well with salt and ground black pepper. Return the chicken to the pan with any juices. Cook for 3 minutes, or until the mushrooms are soft.
3. Stir in the cream and season to taste. Serve over fettuccine or rice.

NUTRITION PER SERVE
Protein 35 g; Fat 20 g; Carbohydrate 2 g; Dietary Fiber 2 g; Cholesterol 95 mg; 335 calories

Chicken bake (top) with Chicken and mushroom sauté

❖ Marvelous Chicken Recipes ❖

❖ **MARVELOUS CHICKEN RECIPES** ❖

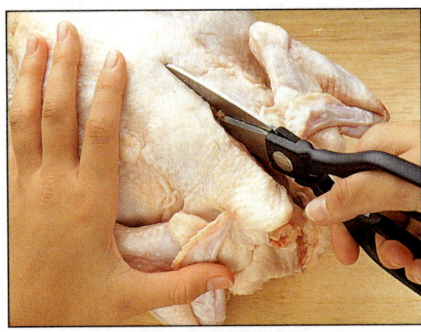

1 Cut the chicken in half along the back with a pair of poultry shears.

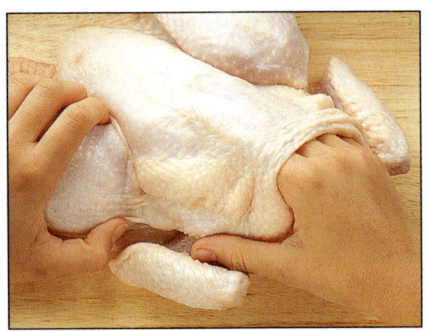

2 Loosen the skin by sliding a hand between the flesh and the skin.

Moroccan butterflied chicken

Preparation time:
15 minutes
Total cooking time:
1 hour
Serves 4

1 x 3 lb chicken
1 tablespoon olive oil
1 1/2 teaspoons ground cumin
1 1/2 teaspoons ground coriander

Olive and lemon stuffing
2 tablespoons finely chopped preserved lemon, rind only
1/4 cup chopped pitted green olives
1/4 cup pine nuts
2 tablespoons chopped fresh flat-leaf parsley
1 teaspoon harissa

1. Preheat the oven to 350°F. Tuck the wings underneath the chicken, then split the chicken down the length of the back with a pair of poultry shears. Open the chicken out and flatten it down with your hands.
2. To make the olive and lemon stuffing, place the preserved lemon rind, olives, pine nuts, parsley and harissa in a bowl and mix well to combine.
3. Loosen the skin covering the chicken breast and legs by sliding a hand between the flesh and the skin. Push the stuffing under the skin, working it across the breast and down to the legs. Skewer the legs to the side of the body.
4. Brush the chicken lightly with the oil. Combine the ground cumin and ground coriander and sprinkle over the chicken.
5. Place the chicken on a rack in a roasting pan and roast for 1 hour. Test for doneness by inserting a skewer into a thigh. If the juices that run out are clear, then the chicken is cooked. If the juices are pink, bake the chicken for another 10 minutes before testing again.
6. When cooked, remove the chicken from the oven and allow to rest in a warm place for 10 minutes before carving into portions. Serve with steamed couscous or saffron rice and a leafy green salad.

NUTRITION PER SERVE
Protein 60 g; Fat 15 g; Carbohydrate 3 g; Dietary Fiber 2 g; Cholesterol 125 mg; 395 calories

Note: Harissa is a fiery chili paste, available in Middle Eastern markets.

Moroccan butterflied chicken

3 Push the stuffing under the skin, working it down to the legs.

4 Skewer the chicken legs to the body to help it hold its shape.

Roast chicken with garlic and potatoes

Preparation time:
  35 minutes
Total cooking time:
  55 minutes.
Serves 4

2 lb 8 oz chicken pieces
4 floury potatoes, unpeeled and cut into large chunks
2 tablespoons coarsely chopped fresh rosemary
1 tablespoon fresh lemon thyme leaves
1/2 cup olive oil
1/4 cup chicken stock
1 whole head of garlic, broken into cloves

1. Preheat the oven to 400°F. Place the chicken pieces, potatoes, herbs, oil and plenty of salt and pepper in a roasting pan.
2. Toss well and bake for 30 minutes, turning regularly and brushing the stock over the chicken to moisten. Scatter the garlic over the top and bake for another 15–20 minutes.
3. Serve the chicken with the garlic, potatoes and the juices and oil poured over.

NUTRITION PER SERVE
Protein 45 g; Fat 35 g; Carbohydrate 15 g; Dietary Fiber 3.5 g; Cholesterol 90 mg; 550 calories

Chicken schnitzels Florentine

Preparation time:
  30 minutes
Total cooking time:
  45 minutes
Serves 4

Tomato Sauce
1 tablespoon olive oil
1 onion, finely chopped
2 cloves garlic, crushed
16 oz can crushed tomatoes
1/4 cup white wine or water
1 teaspoon sugar
1/2 teaspoon dried oregano

1 lb young spinach, washed, drained and stems removed
1/4 cup whipping cream
4 skinless, boned chicken breast halves, tenderloins removed
flour, for coating
1/4 cup butter
1 tablespoon olive oil
3/4 cup shredded Gruyère or Cheddar

1. To make the tomato sauce, heat the oil in a saucepan. Add the onion and garlic. Cook for 5 minutes until soft. Add the tomatoes, wine, sugar and oregano and cook for 15 minutes over low heat until thick and reduced.
2. Coarsely chop the spinach and place in a skillet. Cook over medium heat for 2–3 minutes, or until it is wilted. Cool and squeeze dry. Fold in the cream and season.
3. Trim the chicken of any excess fat or sinew, pat dry and place each piece between 2 sheets of plastic wrap. Using a mallet or rolling pin, gently flatten out to 5/8 inch thick.
4. Lightly coat the chicken with the flour and shake off any excess. Heat the butter and oil in a large heavy-based skillet. Cook the schnitzels for 2 minutes each side, or until lightly browned.
5. Top each schnitzel with the spinach and cheese. Pour the tomato sauce around the chicken, taking care not to cover the cheese.
6. Cover the pan and cook over low heat for 10–15 minutes, or until the cheese has melted.

NUTRITION PER SERVE
Protein 45 g; Fat 35 g; Carbohydrate 10 g; Dietary Fiber 5.5 g; Cholesterol 135 mg; 540 calories

---

Roast chicken with garlic and potatoes (top) with Chicken schnitzels Florentine

❖ MARVELOUS CHICKEN RECIPES ❖

❖ MARVELOUS CHICKEN RECIPES ❖

Chicken paella

Preparation time:
30 minutes
Total cooking time:
1 hour
Serves 4–6

2 tomatoes
4 chicken thighs, with skin on
1/4 cup olive oil, for frying
2 oz chorizo sausage, cut into 1/4 inch slices
2 cloves garlic, crushed
1 red onion, sliced
2 cups short-grain rice
1 red sweet bell pepper, cut into thin strips
3 cups chicken stock
1/8 teaspoon saffron threads
1 cup frozen peas
12 green mussels, scrubbed and beards removed
8 raw shrimp, shelled and deveined with tails intact
8 oz squid (calamari) tubes, cut into 1/2 inch rings

1. Score a cross on the base of the tomatoes, place in a bowl and cover with boiling water for 10 seconds. Plunge into cold water, peel, seed and chop.

2. Cut the chicken in half along the bone, keeping the bone attached to one side. Pierce the skin. Heat the oil in a large skillet over high heat. Brown the chicken for 10 minutes, then drain on paper towels. Fry the chorizo for 2–3 minutes; drain on paper towels.
3. Add the garlic and onion and cook for 5 minutes. Add the rice and stir for 1–2 minutes until coated with oil. Add the tomatoes, chicken, chorizo and red pepper, reduce the heat and cook for 5 minutes.
4. Bring the stock, 1 cup water and the saffron to a boil in a saucepan, then pour over the rice and simmer over very low heat for 10 minutes. Stir in the peas and cook, covered, for 10 minutes. Add the mussels, shrimp and squid and cook, uncovered, for 10 minutes, or until all the liquid is absorbed. Do not stir at this stage as it should form a thin crust on the base.

NUTRITION PER SERVE (6)
Protein 40 g; Fat 15 g; Carbohydrate 60 g; Dietary Fiber 4 g; Cholesterol 185 mg; 570 calories

Smoked chicken and mustard linguine

Preparation time:
10 minutes
Total cooking time:
15 minutes
Serves 6

1 lb linguine
1 smoked or plain cooked chicken
1 1/4 cups sour cream
1 tablespoon coarse-grain mustard
1 tablespoon chopped fresh flat-leaf parsley, to garnish

1. Bring a large saucepan of salted water to a boil and cook the linguine until *al dente*. Drain the pasta, reserving 1/2 cup water in case you need to thin the sauce.
2. Remove all the meat from the chicken and discard the skin and bones. Slice into pieces.
3. Place the sour cream in a skillet and warm it over low heat until it thins. Stir in the mustard, chicken and salt and pepper.
4. Toss the linguine into the sauce and mix well. Sprinkle with parsley.

NUTRITION PER SERVE
Protein 50 g; Fat 45 g; Carbohydrate 60 g; Dietary Fiber 4 g; Cholesterol 205 mg; 875 calories

---

Chicken paella (top) with Smoked chicken and mustard linguine

Tandoori chicken

Preparation time:
  10 minutes + overnight refrigeration
Total cooking time:
  30 minutes
Serves 6–8

8 chicken drumsticks
8 chicken thighs
juice of 1 lemon
1 onion, finely chopped
2 cloves garlic, crushed
1 tablespoon grated fresh ginger
1–2 red chiles
1 tablespoon garam masala
1 teaspoon paprika
1/4 teaspoon salt
2 cups plain yogurt
red and yellow food colors
lemon wedges, to serve

1. Cut 3 slits in each piece of chicken and place in a bowl with the lemon juice; mix well.
2. Place the onion, garlic, ginger, chiles, garam masala, paprika, salt and yogurt in a blender and blend until smooth. Add the food colors until you have the color you want and pour the mixture over the chicken. Cover and refrigerate overnight.
3. Preheat the oven to its highest setting. Lift the chicken out of the marinade and drain off any excess. Place on a wire rack in a roasting pan and cook for 20–30 minutes (the drumsticks may take a little longer), or until they have a charred appearance around the edges. Serve with the lemon wedges.

NUTRITION PER SERVE (8)
Protein 45 g; Fat 8.5 g; Carbohydrate 4 g; Dietary Fiber 0 g; Cholesterol 120 mg; 270 calories

Spicy chicken and chickpea bake

Preparation time:
  30 minutes
Total cooking time:
  1 hour 10 minutes
Serves 4–6

1 teaspoon cumin seeds, lightly crushed
1 tablespoon coriander seeds, lightly crushed
1 tablespoon olive oil
3 lb chicken pieces
1 green sweet bell pepper, seeded and cut into large cubes
2 onions, thickly sliced
2 cloves garlic, chopped
1 green chile, seeded and chopped
1/2 teaspoon saffron threads
3/4 cup basmati rice
1 1/2 cups chicken stock
1/2 cup white wine
grated rind and juice of a lemon
10 oz can chickpeas, drained
1/3 cup green olives

1. Preheat the oven to 350°F. Place a 16-cup flameproof casserole or Dutch oven on the stove. Dry-fry the cumin and coriander seeds for 1 minute until aromatic; set aside.
2. Heat the oil in the casserole. Add the chicken in 2 batches and fry for 3–4 minutes over high heat, turning, until well browned. Remove.
3. Add the green pepper, onions, garlic and chile to the casserole and stir for 3–4 minutes, without coloring. Stir in the saffron, rice and spices and cook for 1 minute.
4. Add the chicken stock, wine, lemon rind and juice. Slowly bring to a boil, stirring, then remove from the heat and place the chicken on top. Bake, covered, for 45 minutes until the rice is cooked. Stir in the drained chickpeas and olives and bake for another 5 minutes.

NUTRITION PER SERVE (6)
Protein 45 g; Fat 8.5 g; Carbohydrate 30 g; Dietary Fiber 4.5 g; Cholesterol 85 mg; 395 calories

Tandoori chicken (top) with Spicy chicken and chickpea bake

❖ MARVELOUS CHICKEN RECIPES ❖

❖ Marvelous Chicken Recipes ❖

❖ MARVELOUS CHICKEN RECIPES ❖

Pesto chicken

Preparation time:
20 minutes
Total cooking time:
25 minutes
Serves 4

1 cup firmly packed basil leaves
1/4 cup pine nuts, toasted
1/4 cup grated Parmesan
1/4 cup olive oil
4 skinless, boned chicken breast halves
2 teaspoons oil, extra
2 teaspoons butter
1 small onion, finely chopped
1 clove garlic, crushed
1/2 cup white wine
3/4 cup chicken stock
1 tablespoon pine nuts, toasted, extra

1. Process the basil, pine nuts and Parmesan until fine. With the motor running, gradually add the oil to form a smooth paste and season.
2. Trim the chicken of any excess fat or sinew. Heat the extra oil and butter in a skillet, add the chicken and cook over a high heat until browned. Remove from the pan and let cool slightly. Cut 4 deep slashes across the chicken, three quarters of the way through. Fill each slash with a teaspoon of the pesto.
3. Cook the onion and garlic for 5 minutes until soft. Add the wine and chicken stock, bring to a boil, then reduce the heat and simmer for 5 minutes. Return the chicken to the pan, pesto-side-up, and simmer, partly covered, for 8–10 minutes. Sprinkle with the extra pine nuts.

NUTRITION PER SERVE
Protein 40 g; Fat 35 g; Carbohydrate 2.5 g; Dietary Fiber 1.5 g; Cholesterol 85 mg; 495 calories

Chicken Parmigiana

Preparation time:
25 minutes +
30 minutes chilling
Total cooking time:
35 minutes
Serves 4

4 skinless, boned chicken breast halves
seasoned flour, for coating
dry bread crumbs, for coating
1 egg, lightly beaten
1 tablespoon milk
oil, for frying
1 cup ready-made tomato pasta sauce
2 tablespoons shredded fresh basil leaves
1/2 cup grated Parmesan
4 oz mozzarella cheese, thinly sliced

1. Trim the chicken breast halves of any excess fat or sinew and pat dry with paper towels. Place between sheets of plastic wrap and flatten with a meat mallet or rolling pin to 1/4 inch thick.
2. Place the seasoned flour and bread crumbs on 2 plates. Combine the egg and milk in a shallow bowl. Coat the chicken in the flour, shaking off any excess, dip in the egg and milk, drain and coat in the bread crumbs. Chill for 30 minutes.
3. Preheat the oven to 350°F. Heat 1 1/4 inches of oil in a skillet. Add the crumbed chicken and cook for 3–4 minutes on each side until golden. Drain on paper towels. Place in a single layer in a greased shallow baking dish.
4. Spoon the combined tomato pasta sauce and basil over the chicken, sprinkle with the Parmesan and lay the mozzarella on top. Bake for 20–25 minutes until golden.

NUTRITION PER SERVE
Protein 40 g; Fat 25 g; Carbohydrate 15 g; Dietary Fiber 1.5 g; Cholesterol 145 mg; 465 calories

Pesto chicken (top) with Chicken Parmigiana

Chicken dim sums

Preparation time:
  30 minutes
Total cooking time:
  45 minutes
Makes about 60

1 egg white
1 tablespoon cornstarch
2 tablespoons soy sauce
1 teaspoon sesame oil
1 lb skinless, boned chicken thighs, coarsely chopped
4 oz baby bok choy (Chinese white cabbage), finely chopped
1/3 cup chopped canned water chestnuts
1/4 cup finely chopped green onions
2 tablespoons finely chopped cilantro
2 teaspoons finely grated fresh ginger
8 oz won ton skins

Dipping Sauce
1/4 cup soy sauce
1/4 cup water
1 tablespoon fresh lime juice

1. Place the egg white in a large bowl and beat lightly. Whisk in the cornstarch, soy sauce and sesame oil.
2. Place the chicken thighs in a food processor and process until finely chopped. Stir into the egg white mixture with the baby bok choy, water chestnuts, green onions, cilantro and ginger. Mix the ingredients thoroughly and season with salt.
3. Working with 1 won ton skin at a time, place 2 teaspoons of the mixture onto the center of each wrapper. Gather the skin up to the center like a pouch, leaving the top open, and gently press the filling down to firmly pack. Tap on the bench to flatten the base.
4. Brush a steamer lightly with oil and place the dim sums in a single layer (they will need to be cooked in batches). Bring a pan of water to a boil and place the steamer on top. Cover and steam for about 15 minutes per batch.
5. To make the dipping sauce, place the soy sauce, water and lime juice in a small bowl and stir to combine. Serve with the warm dim sums.

NUTRITION PER SERVE
Protein 1 g; Fat 0.5 g; Carbohydrate 4 g; Dietary Fiber 0.5 g; Cholesterol 4 mg; 20 calories

Note: Steamers often have more than one layer, so it is possible to steam more than one batch at a time.

Chicken dim sums

1 Chop the baby bok choy and the water chestnuts.

2 Place 2 level teaspoons of the mixture on the center of each won ton skin.

❖ Marvelous Chicken Recipes ❖

3 Gather up the pastry to make a dim sum shape, leaving the top open.

4 Place the dim sums in a steamer, cover and steam for 15 minutes.

31

Mediterranean sauté

Preparation time:
  20 minutes
Total cooking time:
  25 minutes
Serves 4

4 skinless, boned
  chicken breast halves
1/4 cup flour
2 tablespoons butter
1 tablespoon olive oil
2 cloves garlic, chopped
16 oz can crushed
  tomatoes
1 tablespoon chopped
  fresh oregano
1 tablespoon chopped
  fresh sage
2 tablespoons dry white
  wine
1/2 red sweet bell
  pepper, sliced
4 oz pitted black olives
2 oz feta cheese,
  crumbled
fresh oregano leaves, to
  garnish

1. Trim the chicken and coat lightly in flour, shaking off any excess.
2. Heat the butter, oil and garlic in a skillet until foamy. Fry the chicken for 3 minutes each side until brown.
3. Stir in the tomatoes, herbs and wine, season and sprinkle with the red pepper and olives. Partially cover, simmer for 10–15 minutes, then top with the feta and oregano leaves to serve.

NUTRITION PER SERVE
Protein 40 g; Fat 20 g; Carbohydrate 10 g; Dietary Fiber 3 g; Cholesterol 105 mg; 375 calories

Chicken terrine

Preparation time:
  30 minutes +
  overnight refrigeration
Total cooking time:
  1 hour 40 minutes
Serves 8–10

3 tablespoons butter
1 large onion, finely
  chopped
2 cloves garlic, crushed
10–14 bacon slices
2 lb ground chicken
1/2 cup whipping cream
1 egg, lightly beaten
1/3 cup pistachio nuts,
  shelled
1 cup fresh soft bread
  crumbs
1 tablespoon fresh
  rosemary leaves
1 skinless, boned
  chicken breast half

1. Preheat the oven to 350°F. Grease an 8 1/2 x 5 1/2 inch loaf pan and line with parchment paper or foil.
2. Melt the butter in a skillet, add the onion and garlic and cook over low heat for 5–10 minutes, without coloring. Cool.
3. Line the loaf pan with enough bacon to cover the base and sides, leaving it to hang over the edges.
4. In a bowl, combine the onion mixture with the ground chicken, cream, egg, pistachios, bread crumbs, rosemary and salt and pepper. Fry a small piece and taste for seasoning.
5. Trim the chicken breast and cut into 6 strips. Press a third of the chicken mixture into the pan and lay 3 chicken strips lengthwise over it. Repeat with another third of the mixture and chicken strips, and finish with a layer of mixture. Fold the bacon over the top and cover with foil.
6. Place the pan in a baking dish and add boiling water to come halfway up its sides. Bake for 1 1/2 hours, or until the juices run clear when a skewer is inserted. Remove from the dish, cover with plastic wrap and foil and place a similar size pan on top. Place cans on top to weigh down the terrine and chill overnight. Invert the pan, remove the paper, then cut into thick slices. Serve with a relish.

NUTRITION PER SERVE (10)
Protein 15 g; Fat 15 g; Carbohydrate 8 g; Dietary Fiber 1 g; Cholesterol 70 mg; 215 calories

Mediterranean sauté (top) with Chicken terrine

❖ Marvelous Chicken Recipes ❖

❖ Marvelous Chicken Recipes ❖

Macadamia-crusted chicken

Preparation time:
30 minutes + 1 hour refrigeration
Total cooking time:
25 minutes
Serves 4

4 skinless, boned chicken breast halves
2 tablespoons cranberry sauce
4 oz Camembert cheese, mashed
seasoned flour, to coat
1 egg, lightly beaten
1 tablespoon milk
1 cup fresh soft bread crumbs
1 1/4 cups macadamia nuts, finely chopped

1. Preheat the oven to 400°F. Trim the chicken of any excess fat or sinew, then cut a deep pocket in the side of each breast. Spread 2 teaspoons of cranberry sauce inside the pocket and fill with Camembert. Secure the opening with a cocktail pick.
2. Place the flour on a plate, the combined egg and milk in a shallow bowl and the combined bread crumbs and nuts on a plate. Coat the chicken in flour, shaking off any excess, then dip in the egg and milk and coat with the bread crumbs and nuts. Refrigerate for 1 hour.
3. Place the chicken breasts in a single layer in a greased baking dish. Bake for 20–25 minutes, or until golden brown. Remove the cocktail picks.

NUTRITION PER SERVE
Protein 45 g; Fat 50 g; Carbohydrate 20 g; Dietary Fiber 5 g; Cholesterol 145 mg; 715 calories

Chicken fajitas

Preparation time:
35 minutes + 2 hours marinating
Total cooking time:
20 minutes
Serves 4–6

Marinade
1/2 cup lime juice
4 cloves garlic, crushed
2 tablespoons oil
1/2 teaspoon salt
1/2 teaspoon black pepper

1 lb 4 oz skinless, boned chicken breast halves, cut into thin diagonal strips
4 flour tortillas
2 tablespoons oil
2 red onions, thinly sliced
1 red sweet bell pepper, thinly sliced
1 green sweet bell pepper, thinly sliced

1. To make the marinade, combine the ingredients in a nonreactive bowl.
2. Trim the chicken of any excess fat or sinew and toss in the marinade. Cover and refrigerate for 2 hours.
3. Preheat the oven to 350°F. Wrap the tortillas in aluminum foil and bake for 10 minutes to soften. Keep warm.
4. Heat half the oil in a cast-iron or heavy-based skillet. Drain the chicken from the marinade and cook, in batches, over high heat for 4–5 minutes, or until charred and cooked through. Remove and keep warm. Add the remaining oil and cook the vegetables for 3 minutes.
5. Working with one tortilla at a time (and leaving the other tortillas wrapped up as you work), place a quarter of the chicken along the center of the tortilla, top with a quarter of the vegetables and roll up to encase the filling. Repeat with the remaining tortillas and filling. Serve with guacamole and a fresh tomato salsa.

NUTRITION PER SERVE (6)
Protein 25 g; Fat 15 g; Carbohydrate 5 g; Dietary Fiber 1 g; Cholesterol 85 mg; 200 calories

---

Macadamia-crusted chicken (top) with Chicken fajitas

Marvelous Chicken Recipes

Crusted chicken with corn salsa

Preparation time:
  35 minutes
  + 30 minutes soaking
Total cooking time:
  40 minutes
Serves 4

2 lb chicken pieces
1 1/2 cups milk
1/2 cup cornmeal
1/2 cup all-purpose flour
1/2 teaspoon paprika
1/2 teaspoon curry powder
1/8 teaspoon cayenne pepper
oil, for frying

Salsa
1 cup fresh corn kernels, lightly blanched (or use frozen)
1 tomato, diced
2 green onions, thinly sliced
1 tablespoon finely chopped cilantro
2 tablespoons sour cream

1. In a bowl, soak the chicken pieces in the milk for 30 minutes. In a separate bowl, combine the cornmeal, flour, paprika, curry powder, cayenne pepper and some salt and ground black pepper.
2. Drain the chicken gently before coating with the cornmeal and spice mixture.
3. In a large skillet, heat 3/4 inch of the oil to 350°F. Add the chicken in batches and cook on all sides for 17–20 minutes, or until cooked through and golden. Drain on paper towels.
4. To make the salsa, combine the ingredients. Serve with the chicken.

NUTRITION PER SERVE
Protein 50 g; Fat 15 g; Carbohydrate 50 g; Dietary Fiber 4 g; Cholesterol 115 mg; 510 calories

Rosemary chicken fingers on bruschetta

Preparation time:
  25 minutes
Total cooking time:
  15 minutes
Serves 4

Lemon mayonnaise
2/3 cup mayonnaise
2 tablespoons sour cream
1 tablespoon chopped fresh parsley
2 teaspoons grated fresh lemon rind

4 skinless, boned chicken breast halves
1/4 cup light olive oil
1 tablespoon chopped fresh rosemary
1 French baguette, cut into thick diagonal slices
several butter lettuce leaves
fresh rosemary sprigs, to garnish

1. To make the lemon mayonnaise, combine all the ingredients with some black pepper. Mix well and set aside.
2. Trim the chicken of any excess fat or sinew and cut into long thin strips. Place in a bowl with half the oil, rosemary and salt and pepper; toss well.
3. Heat a cast-iron barbecue griddle plate or heavy-based skillet until smoking hot, then brush lightly with a little oil. Cook the chicken in batches, searing until golden brown and just tender. Set aside.
4. Toast the bread and brush with the remaining oil. To serve, place a lettuce leaf on each bruschetta. Place a few strips of chicken in the lettuce and drizzle with the lemon mayonnaise. Garnish with the rosemary sprigs.

NUTRITION PER SERVE
Protein 50 g; Fat 55 g; Carbohydrate 70 g; Dietary Fiber 5 g; Cholesterol 100 mg; 945 calories

Crusted chicken with corn salsa (top) and Rosemary chicken fingers on bruschetta

❖ Marvelous Chicken Recipes ❖

❖ MARVELOUS CHICKEN RECIPES ❖

Chicken pizza

Preparation time:
20 minutes
Total cooking time:
20 minutes
Serves 2–4

1 red onion,
 sliced
1 cup sour cream
1 clove garlic,
 crushed
2 teaspoons chopped
 fresh thyme
1/4 cup grated
 Parmesan
1 cup cubed cooked
 or barbecued
 chicken
1 large ready-made
 pizza base
1 large open, flat
 mushroom, thinly
 sliced
fi cup cubed
 mozzarella
1 teaspoon chopped
 fresh thyme leaves

1. Preheat the oven to 400°F. Mix the red onion, sour cream, garlic, thyme and Parmesan together and set aside. Season the chicken with salt and black pepper.
2. Place the pizza base on a baking sheet and spread it with the onion mixture. Top with the mushroom, chicken and mozzarella. Bake for 15–20 minutes, or until the cheese is golden. Sprinkle with the chopped thyme.

NUTRITION PER SERVE (4)
Protein 30 g; Fat 35 g; Carbohydrate 4 g; Dietary Fiber 1 g; Cholesterol 170 mg; 450 calories

Chicken stroganoff balls

Preparation time:
15 minutes
Total cooking time:
20 minutes
Serves 4

1 lb ground chicken
2 cloves garlic,
 crushed
1 small onion,
 grated
seasoned flour, to coat
2 tablespoons oil
2 tablespoons butter
1 large onion,
 sliced
6 oz button
 mushrooms, halved
1 tablespoon sweet
 paprika
1 tablespoon tomato
 paste
2 teaspoons Dijon
 mustard
1/2 cup white wine
1/3 cup chicken
 stock
3/4 cup sour cream
2 tablespoons chopped
 fresh parsley

Chicken pizza (top) with Chicken stroganoff balls

1. Combine the ground chicken, garlic and grated onion in a bowl. Using your hands, mix well. Roll level tablespoons of the mixture into balls with lightly floured hands. Place the seasoned flour on a piece of waxed paper and carefully roll the balls in the flour, shaking off the excess.
2. Heat half the oil and butter in a skillet. Cook the balls in batches over medium heat, shaking the pan frequently until brown and adding more oil when necessary. Drain on paper towels.
3. Heat the remaining oil and butter in the pan. Add the sliced onion and cook over medium heat for 3–4 minutes. Add the mushrooms and paprika and stir for 1–2 minutes. Stir in the combined tomato paste, mustard, wine and stock. Bring to a boil, reduce the heat and simmer for 5 minutes. Stir in the sour cream. Return the balls to the pan and stir until heated through. Season with salt and pepper and sprinkle with parsley. Serve with pasta.

NUTRITION PER SERVE
Protein 33 g; Fat 35 g; Carbohydrate 6 g; Dietary Fiber 3 g; Cholesterol 140 mg; 510 calories

Thai green curry

Preparation time:
 20 minutes
Total cooking time:
 35 minutes
Serves 4

1 tablespoon oil
2 tablespoons Thai green curry paste
1 1/2 cups unsweetened coconut cream
1 lb 4 oz skinless, boned chicken thighs, cut into bite-size pieces
7 oz can bamboo shoots, drained
1 tablespoon fish sauce
6 Kaffir lime leaves
2 teaspoons palm sugar or soft brown sugar
1 stalk lemon grass, white part only
2 teaspoons green peppercorns, drained
6 oz yard-long beans, cut into short lengths
1/2 cup Thai basil leaves

1. Heat the oil in a wok or heavy-based saucepan. Add the curry paste and cook until fragrant. Add the coconut cream and 1 cup water. Bring to a boil, stirring, and cook for 10 minutes over high heat until oil bubbles break the surface.
2. Add the chicken, bamboo shoots, fish sauce, lime leaves and sugar. Lightly bruise the lemon grass with the back of a knife and add. Simmer for 10 minutes, stirring occasionally. Add the peppercorns and beans and cook for 10 minutes, or until the sauce has thickened.
3. Remove the lime leaves and lemon grass and stir in the basil.

NUTRITION PER SERVE
Protein 40 g; Fat 35 g; Carbohydrate 10 g; Dietary Fiber 4 g; Cholesterol 75 mg; 520 calories

Note: Green curry paste, fish sauce (nam pla), kaffir lime leaves, palm sugar (jaggery), lemon grass and Thai basil leaves can be found at Southeast Asian markets.

Vietnamese noodle salad

Preparation time:
 40 minutes
Total cooking time:
 10 minutes
Serves 4

Dressing
2/3 cup fresh lime juice
2 tablespoons rice or white vinegar
1/3 cup fish sauce
2 tablespoons soft brown sugar
2 red onions, thinly sliced
6 oz cellophane (mung bean) noodles
2 large skinless, boned chicken breast halves
2 small carrots, peeled into ribbons
2 short, thin cucumbers, peeled into ribbons
1/2 cup cilantro leaves
1 cup fresh mint leaves
8 iceberg lettuce leaves, shredded
1/3 cup coarsely chopped unsalted peanuts
chile flakes, to garnish

1. To make the dressing, place the ingredients in a bowl and whisk with a fork. Cover and set aside.
2. Place the noodles in a heatproof bowl and cover with boiling water. Soak for 5 minutes, rinse and drain. Cut into short lengths and add to the dressing.
3. Trim the chicken, then remove the tenderloins and steam with the breasts for 10 minutes until cooked. Shred the chicken using 2 forks and mix into the dressing with the vegetables and herbs.
4. Divide the lettuce among 4 plates. Fill with the mixture, then sprinkle with the peanuts and chile.

NUTRITION PER SERVE
Protein 25 g; Fat 8 g; Carbohydrate 60 g; Dietary Fiber 5.5 g; Cholesterol 40 mg; 430 calories

Thai green curry (top) and Vietnamese noodle salad

❖ Marvelous Chicken Recipes ❖

❖ **Marvelous Chicken Recipes** ❖

Chicken, prosciutto and semi-dried tomato salad

Preparation time:
 25 minutes + 20 minutes marinating
Total cooking time:
 15 minutes
Serves 4

4 skinless, boned chicken breast halves
1 tablespoon olive oil
2 teaspoons lemon juice
1 clove garlic, crushed
4 slices prosciutto
6 oz mixed salad leaves
16 semi-dried tomatoes
1/3 cup pine nuts, toasted
1/4 cup fresh basil leaves

Dressing
1/4 cup olive oil
1 tablespoon balsamic vinegar
1 teaspoon Dijon mustard
1 teaspoon honey

1. Trim the chicken of any excess fat or sinew and marinate in the combined oil, juice and garlic for 20 minutes. Chargrill or broil for 10 minutes, then thinly slice on the diagonal. Dry-fry the prosciutto in a hot skillet until it is crispy and break into large pieces.
2. To make the dressing, place all the ingredients in a jar and shake well.
3. Place the salad leaves on 4 plates and arrange the chicken, tomatoes, pine nuts, basil and prosciutto on top. Drizzle with dressing.

NUTRITION PER SERVE
Protein 30 g; Fat 30 g; Carbohydrate 3 g; Dietary Fiber 1 g; Cholesterol 70 mg; 415 calories

Family chicken gratin

Preparation time:
 20 minutes
Total cooking time:
 35 minutes
Serves 4

3 tablespoons butter
1 onion, chopped
2 cloves garlic, crushed
2 slices bacon, chopped
1/2 red sweet bell pepper, chopped
1 stalk celery, chopped
1/4 cup all-purpose flour
2 1/2 cups milk
2 cups chopped cooked or barbecued chicken (see Note)
3 cups cold cooked brown or white rice
1 cup shredded Cheddar
1/2 cup finely shredded Parmesan

1. Preheat an oven to 350° F. Grease a 10-cup baking dish.
2. Heat the butter in a large saucepan. Cook the onion, garlic and bacon for 2–3 minutes, or until soft but not browned. Add the red pepper and celery and continue to cook for 2–3 minutes.
3. Stir in the flour and cook for 1 minute, then gradually add the milk, stirring constantly until the mixture is smooth and thick. Simmer for another 2–3 minutes to allow the flour to cook. Stir in the chopped chicken.
4. Place the rice in a layer over the bottom of the prepared dish. Pour in the chicken mixture and smooth the surface with a spatula. Sprinkle with the Cheddar and Parmesan.
5. Bake for 25 minutes, or until the gratin is bubbling and browned. Serve at once.

NUTRITION PER SERVE
Protein 50 g; Fat 35 g; Carbohydrate 60 g; Dietary Fiber 3 g; Cholesterol 175 mg; 757 calories

Note: Half a cooked or barbecued chicken will yield about 2 cups of chicken meat.

Chicken, prosciutto and semi-dried tomato salad (top) with Family chicken gratin

❖ MARVELOUS CHICKEN RECIPES ❖

Chicken liver pâté

Preparation time:
10 minutes +
overnight refrigeration
Total cooking time:
15 minutes
Serves 4–6

1 onion, finely
  chopped
1/3 cup butter,
  melted
1 clove garlic,
  crushed
1 tablespoon chopped
  fresh thyme
1 lb chicken livers,
  cleaned
2 teaspoons green
  peppercorns, drained
  and coarsely chopped
1 tablespoon brandy
1/2 cup clarified butter
  or ghee
green peppercorns and
  fresh thyme, to
  decorate

1. Cook the onion in 2 tablespoons of the butter until soft. Add the garlic and thyme and cook for 1 minute, then add the livers to the pan and cook for 10 minutes, or until cooked through and firm to the touch.
2. Put the mixture in a food processor or blender and add the rest of the butter. Blend until smooth; season. Add the peppercorns and brandy and blend briefly to mix.
3. Spoon into four 1/2-cup ramekins or a pâté dish and cover with plastic wrap, pressing the plastic wrap onto the surface of the pâté. Refrigerate the pâté overnight.
4. Cover the pâté with the clarified butter or ghee and decorate with peppercorns and thyme.

NUTRITION PER SERVE (6)
*Protein 20 g; Fat 25 g;
Carbohydrate 1.5 g; Dietary
Fiber 1 g; Cholesterol
65 mg; 200 calories*

Chicken with salad greens and chèvre cheese

Preparation time:
20 minutes + 20
minutes marinating
Total cooking time:
10 minutes
Serves 4

3 skinless, boned
  chicken breast halves
1 tablespoon olive oil
2 teaspoons lemon juice
1 butter lettuce, outer
  leaves removed
1 curly endive, outer
  leaves removed
1 small romaine lettuce,
  outer leaves removed
2 oz arugula leaves,
  lower stems removed
1 cup seedless green
  grapes
4 oz cherry tomatoes,
  halved
1/2 cup chopped pecans
5 oz firm chèvre cheese,
  cubed
1 tablespoon chopped
  fresh chives

Mustard Honey Dressing
1/4 cup olive oil
1 tablespoon lemon
  juice
2 teaspoons coarse-
  grain mustard
1 teaspoon honey

1. Trim the chicken of any excess fat or sinew and marinate in the combined oil and lemon juice for at least 20 minutes. Chargrill or broil the chicken for about 10 minutes, then cut into 3/4 inch cubes.
2. To make the dressing, place the ingredients in a jar and shake to combine.
3. Wash and dry the salad leaves and tear into large pieces. Place in a serving bowl, then add the chicken cubes, grapes, tomato halves, pecans and chèvre.
4. Pour the dressing over the salad and gently toss. Sprinkle with the chives.

NUTRITION PER SERVE
*Protein 35 g; Fat 40 g;
Carbohydrate 10 g; Dietary
Fiber 4 g; Cholesterol
80 mg; 550 calories*

*Chicken liver pâté (top) and
Chicken with salad greens and chèvre cheese*

❖ Marvelous Chicken Recipes ❖

Chicken, sweet pepper and feta rolls

Preparation time:
 25 minutes
Total cooking time:
 25 minutes
Serves 6

6 skinless, boned chicken breast halves
1 red sweet bell pepper
1 yellow sweet bell pepper
4 oz young spinach leaves
2 oz feta cheese
2 tablespoons oil

1. Trim the chicken of any excess fat or sinew, then pat dry with paper towels. Place each breast between 2 sheets of plastic wrap and flatten with a meat mallet or rolling pin to a 1/4 inch thickness.
2. Cut the sweet peppers into large pieces and remove the seeds and membrane. Place on a baking sheet under a preheated broiler until the skin has blackened and blistered. Place in a plastic bag to cool. When the pepper pieces have cooled, peel away the skin. Cut into 1 1/2 inch wide strips.
3. Trim and wash the spinach leaves and place in a saucepan, with just the water clinging to the leaves. Cover and cook over low heat until just wilted. Drain the spinach in a colander and squeeze out any excess liquid by placing the spinach between 2 equal-sized plates and pressing them together.
4. Place the chicken skinned-side-down on a work surface and lay the strips of red and yellow pepper evenly on top of it, close to one end of each breast. Spread the spinach over the peppers, then crumble the feta cheese over the top.
5. Starting at the same end, roll each breast up, encasing the filling. Tie the chicken with string at intervals along the roll to keep it together during cooking. Poke the chicken in at the ends and tie around the chicken lengthwise to keep secure.
6. Heat the oil in a skillet, add the chicken rolls and cook over medium heat, turning frequently, until browned all over and cooked through. Remove the string and cut into 3/4 inch slices. Serve with a mixed green salad.

NUTRITION PER SERVE
Protein 35 g; Fat 10 g; Carbohydrate 1.5 g; Dietary Fiber 1 g; Cholesterol 80 mg; 265 calories

Chicken, sweet pepper and feta rolls

1 Place the chicken in plastic wrap and flatten with a meat mallet or rolling pin.

2 Place the peppers, spinach and feta at one end of the chicken breasts.

❖ MARVELOUS CHICKEN RECIPES ❖

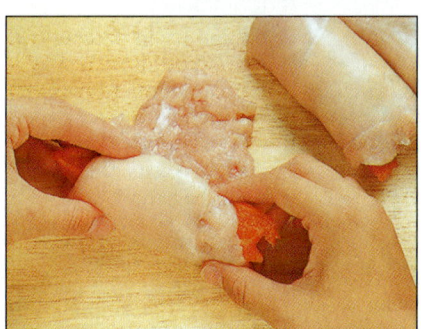

3 Roll up the chicken breasts, starting from the end with the filling.

4 Tie the chicken at intervals along the roll, then tie lengthwise to secure.

47

Baked chicken vermicelli

Preparation time:
  20 minutes
Total cooking time:
  45 minutes
Serves 6

1/2 cup butter
2 onions, finely chopped
12 oz mushrooms, sliced
2 red sweet bell peppers, chopped
1/4 cup flour
1 cup milk
1/2 cup whipping cream
1/2 cup chicken stock
1 large cooked or barbecued chicken
3 chorizo sausages, sliced
10 oz vermicelli
1 cup grated Parmesan

1. Melt half the butter in a skillet and gently fry the onion, mushrooms and red peppers until softened.
2. In a saucepan, melt the remaining butter, stir in the flour and season. Remove from the heat and gradually stir in the milk, cream and stock. Stir until the sauce boils and is thick enough to coat the back of a spoon.
3. Preheat the oven to 350°F. Remove the skin and bones from the chicken; chop the flesh. Add to the sauce with the chorizo and vegetables.
4. Cook the pasta until *al dente*. Drain, then mix with the chicken and half the cheese. Spoon into a baking dish and sprinkle with the rest of the cheese. Cover and bake for 25 minutes.

NUTRITION PER SERVE
Protein 60 g; Fat 60 g; Carbohydrate 50 g; Dietary Fiber 5.5 g; Cholesterol 265 mg; 1105 calories

Chicken Kiev

Preparation time:
  35 minutes
  + 2 hours chilling
Total cooking time:
  20 minutes
Serves 6

1/2 cup butter, softened
1 clove garlic, crushed
2 tablespoons chopped fresh parsley
2 teaspoons lemon juice
2 teaspoons grated lemon rind
6 skinless, boned chicken breast halves, tenderloins removed
1/2 cup all-purpose flour
4 cups dry bread crumbs
2 eggs, beaten
1/4 cup milk
oil, for deep-frying
lemon wedges, to serve

1. Combine the butter, garlic, parsley, lemon juice and rind. Transfer to a sheet of foil and shape into a rectangle about 3 x 2 inches. Fold the foil to encase and chill until firm.
2. Trim the chicken of any excess fat or sinew and place between 2 sheets of plastic wrap. Use a meat mallet or rolling pin to flatten the breasts to about a 1/4 inch thickness.
3. Cut the chilled butter into 6 pieces. Place a piece in the center of each breast, fold in the edges and roll up to encase. Fasten with cocktail picks and chill until firm. Place the flour and bread crumbs on separate plates or waxed paper.
4. Toss the chicken in the flour, dip in the combined egg and milk and coat with the bread crumbs. Chill for 1 hour, then toss in the egg and bread crumbs again. Half fill a heavy-based skillet with oil and fry in batches for 5 minutes on each side until golden and cooked through. Drain on paper towels, remove the cocktail picks and serve with the lemon.

NUTRITION PER SERVE
Protein 40 g; Fat 30 g; Carbohydrate 50 g; Dietary Fiber 3 g; Cholesterol 175 mg; 625 calories

Baked chicken vermicelli (top) with Chicken Kiev

❖ MARVELOUS CHICKEN RECIPES ❖

❖ Marvelous Chicken Recipes ❖

Chicken and herb koftas

Preparation time:
  20 minutes
Total cooking time:
  10 minutes
Serves 4–6

1 lb ground chicken
1 onion, grated
1/4 cup chopped fresh parsley
1 tablespoon chopped garlic chives
1 tablespoon chopped fresh thyme
1 egg, lightly beaten
1/2 cup fresh soft bread crumbs
4 teaspoons butter
1 tablespoon oil
hummus (chickpea dip), to serve
8 pita breads, to serve
tabbouleh, to serve
chili sauce, optional

1. Combine the chicken, onion, herbs, egg, bread crumbs and some salt and pepper in a large bowl and mix well using your hands. Divide the mixture into 8 equal portions.
2. Roll each portion into a sausage shape with lightly floured hands. Melt the butter and oil in a skillet and cook the koftas over medium heat, turning frequently, until they are golden brown and cooked through.
3. To serve, spread the hummus over the pita bread, spoon over the tabbouleh and top with a kofta. Add chili sauce if desired, roll up and serve.

NUTRITION PER SERVE (4)
Protein 35 g; Fat 15 g; Carbohydrate 25 g; Dietary Fiber 3 g; Cholesterol 120 mg; 375 calories

Chicken papaya salad with curry dressing

Preparation time:
  25 minutes + 20 minutes marinating
Total cooking time:
  10 minutes
Serves 4

4 small skinless, boned chicken breast halves
1 tablespoon olive oil
2 teaspoons soy sauce
1 clove garlic, crushed
1 1/2 lb papaya, seeded, peeled and chopped into 3/4 inch cubes
1 red sweet bell pepper, seeded and thinly sliced
1 yellow sweet bell pepper, seeded and thinly sliced
1 small fresh fennel bulb, thinly sliced
1/3 cup macadamia nuts, lightly toasted and chopped
1/3 cup chopped fresh mint
lemon wedges, to serve

Curry Dressing
3/4 cup whole-egg mayonnaise
1 cup plain yogurt
1 teaspoon soy sauce
1/2–1 teaspoon curry powder, to taste

1. Trim the chicken of any excess fat or sinew, then coat with the combined oil, soy sauce and garlic. Marinate for at least 20 minutes. Chargrill or broil the chicken for 3–4 minutes on each side, then thinly slice on the diagonal.
2. To make the curry dressing, combine the mayonnaise, yogurt, soy sauce and curry powder, to taste, in a bowl.
3. Combine the papaya and vegetables in a bowl and fold in half the dressing. Arrange the salad on a plate, top with the chicken and a dollop of the remaining dressing. Sprinkle with the macadamias and mint and serve with lemon wedges.

NUTRITION PER SERVE
Protein 35 g; Fat 20 g; Carbohydrate 15 g; Dietary Fiber 6 g; Cholesterol 75 mg; 370 calories

Chicken and herb koftas (top) and Chicken papaya salad with curry dressing

Golden jeweled couscous

Preparation time:
30 minutes
Total cooking time:
20 minutes
Serves 4

1/4 cup butter
1 tablespoon oil
2 large onions, thinly sliced
2 teaspoons ground cumin
1 teaspoon ground coriander
1 teaspoon paprika
1/2 teaspoon turmeric
1/2 teaspoon cinnamon
10 oz skinless, boned chicken thighs, cut into thin strips
2 cups chicken stock
2 cups couscous
1/3 cup sun-dried sweet bell peppers in oil (or use sun-dried tomatoes), chopped
1/4 cup dried currants
1 carrot, shredded
2 tablespoons pine nuts, toasted
lemon wedges, to serve

1. Melt the butter and oil in a large heavy-based saucepan over medium heat until foamy. Add the onion and spices and cook for 4 minutes, stirring occasionally. Remove from the pan with a slotted spoon.
2. Add the chicken and cook until light brown. Return the onion to the pan with the stock.
3. Cover and bring to a boil. Sprinkle in the couscous and stir well. Cover again, remove from the heat and stand for 3 minutes until the liquid is absorbed.
4. Fluff up the couscous with a fork, stir in the peppers (and any oil), currants and carrot, and season. Sprinkle with the pine nuts and serve with the lemon.

NUTRITION PER SERVE
Protein 25 g; Fat 25 g; Carbohydrate 55 g; Dietary Fiber 4 g; Cholesterol 70 mg; 535 calories

Tarragon chicken

Preparation time:
25 minutes
Total cooking time:
1 hour
Serves 4

8 chicken pieces, about 2 lb 6 oz
4 teaspoons butter
1 tablespoon oil
8 cloves garlic, peeled
1 onion, cut in wedges
2 slices bacon, chopped
1 cup chicken stock
1/4 cup tarragon vinegar
1/4 teaspoon dried tarragon
1 tablespoon cornstarch
1/2 cup whipping cream
1/4 cup fresh tarragon leaves

1. Remove any excess fat from the chicken and pat dry with paper towels. Heat the butter and oil in a Dutch oven. Cook the chicken in batches for 5–8 minutes until browned. Set aside.
2. Add the garlic, onion and bacon to the pan. Cook for 3 minutes until soft but not brown. Add the chicken stock, vinegar and dried tarragon and bring slowly to a boil.
3. Add the chicken. Cover and simmer for 40 minutes, or until the chicken is cooked, then remove the chicken from the pan. Add the combined cornstarch, cream and half the tarragon to the sauce, bring to a boil and stir until smooth and thick. Season with pepper. Return the chicken to the sauce, cover and simmer for 10 minutes. Sprinkle with the remaining tarragon.

NUTRITION PER SERVE
Protein 40 g; Fat 25 g; Carbohydrate 5.5 g; Dietary Fiber 1.5 g; Cholesterol 145 mg; 435 calories

Golden jeweled couscous (top) with Tarragon chicken

❖ MARVELOUS CHICKEN RECIPES ❖

❖ **MARVELOUS CHICKEN RECIPES** ❖

1 Remove the legs from the chicken by cutting around the thigh joint.

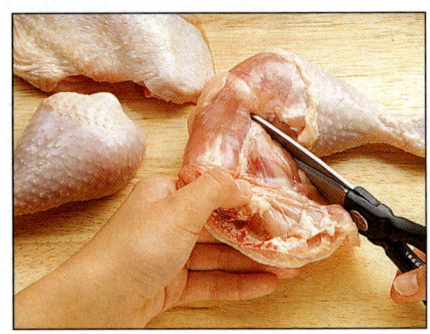

2 Separate the drumstick from the thigh by cutting along the fat line.

54

Coq au vin

Preparation time:
  40 minutes
Total cooking time:
  1 hour 20 minutes
Serves 4

1 x 3 lb chicken
2 tablespoons butter
1 tablespoon oil
12 small boiling
  onions
12 button mushrooms
3 slices bacon,
  chopped
1 carrot, sliced
1 onion, sliced
2 tablespoons brandy
2 cups good-quality red
  wine
3/4 cup chicken stock
1 bouquet garni
2 tablespoons flour
2 tablespoons butter,
  extra

1. Remove the legs from the chicken by cutting around the thigh joint, twisting to break the joint, then cutting through. Separate the thighs from the drumsticks by cutting through the joint along the fat line. Cut up either side of the backbone and discard. Cut lengthwise through the breast bone, then cut each breast in half. Cut off the wing tips through the joint.
2. Heat half the butter and oil in a skillet and cook the onions for 5–8 minutes until brown; remove. Fry the mushrooms and bacon until browned. Set aside.
3. Heat the remaining butter and oil in a Dutch oven, add the carrot and onion and cook over high heat until browned. Set aside. Add the chicken and fry for 5 minutes until golden. Remove the pan from the heat, swirl in the brandy, then add the wine, stock, bouquet garni and carrot and onion mixture. Bring to a boil, reduce the heat and simmer, covered, for 35–40 minutes, or until the chicken is tender. Remove the chicken, strain the sauce and discard the vegetables.
4. Combine the flour and butter to form a paste. Return the sauce to the pan and slowly whisk in the paste. Add the chicken, onions, mushrooms and bacon and simmer for 5–10 minutes to heat through.

NUTRITION PER SERVE
Protein 65 g; Fat 25 g; Carbohydrate 15 g; Dietary Fiber 2.5 g; Cholesterol 185 mg; 660 calories

Note: Make a bouquet garni by placing 2 bay leaves, 2 thyme sprigs, 2 parsley stalks and 6 peppercorns in half a stalk of celery. Cover with the other half and tie firmly with string.

Coq au vin

3 Cut the chicken lengthwise through the breast bone.

4 Your chicken should now be in 8 pieces. Discard the wing tips.

Chicken and sweet potato frittata

Preparation time:
 25 minutes
Total cooking time:
 50 minutes
Serves 4

1 small red sweet bell pepper, seeded and halved
2 tablespoons butter
1 red onion, chopped
2 cloves garlic, crushed
12 oz sweet potato, diced
2 cups chopped young spinach
2 cups chopped cooked or barbecued chicken
4 oz feta cheese, crumbled
1/2 cup chopped fresh basil
6 eggs, lightly beaten

1. Place the red pepper under a preheated broiler. Broil for 8 minutes until blackened, cool, peel, then slice the flesh.
2. Heat the butter in a heavy-based ovenproof skillet, 9 inches across the bottom and 10 inches across the top. Cook the onion and garlic for 2–3 minutes until soft. Add the sweet potato and cook over low heat for 10 minutes, stirring frequently until cooked.
3. Stir in the spinach, chicken, feta, red pepper and basil. Smooth the surface, then pour on the eggs. Cook over low heat for 15 minutes or until almost set.
4. Put the frittata under the broiler. Cook for 10–15 minutes until set. Cut into wedges.

NUTRITION PER SERVE
Protein 40 g; Fat 25 g; Carbohydrate 15 g; Dietary Fiber 3 g; Cholesterol 375 mg; 420 calories

Chicken noodle soup

Preparation time:
 30 minutes
Total cooking time:
 2 hours 15 minutes
Serves 4

Stock
*1 x 3 lb chicken
1 onion, quartered
2 leeks, chopped
2 carrots, chopped
2 bay leaves
small bunch parsley
6 peppercorns
pinch of salt*

*1/2 carrot, diced
1/2 onion, diced
1/2 leek, white part only, chopped
1 cup crushed egg noodles
15 green beans, chopped
1/2 cup frozen peas
1/4 cup chopped fresh parsley*

1. To make the stock, place the ingredients in a large pot with 10 cups cold water. Bring to a boil and skim off any scum from the surface with a slotted spoon. Reduce the heat and simmer for 2 hours. Remove the chicken and set aside to cool. Strain the stock and measure. If it is more than 6 cups, return to the cleaned pot to reduce it. If you are not using the stock immediately, cool and refrigerate overnight (skimming the fat will then be easier because it will solidify). Remove the flesh from the chicken bones and dice it.
2. To make the soup, bring the stock to a boil in a large saucepan and season. Add the carrot, onion and leek and simmer for 3 minutes. Add the noodles and cook for 4–5 minutes. Add the beans, peas and chicken and cook for 3 minutes. Stir in the parsley to serve.

NUTRITION PER SERVE
Protein 70 g; Fat 40 g; Carbohydrate 20 g; Dietary Fiber 5.5 g; Cholesterol 210 mg; 695 calories

Chicken and sweet potato frittata (top) with Chicken noodle soup

❖ MARVELOUS CHICKEN RECIPES ❖

❖ MARVELOUS CHICKEN RECIPES ❖

✣ MARVELOUS CHICKEN RECIPES ✣

Normandy chicken

Preparation time:
  30 minutes
Total cooking time:
  40 minutes
Serves 4

4 skinless, boned chicken breast halves, cut into thick strips
1 tablespoon olive oil
1 clove garlic, crushed
4 green apples
1/4 cup butter
2 tablespoons lemon juice
1 tablespoon brown sugar
1/4 cup Calvados or brandy
1/3 cup whipping cream
4 slices prosciutto
1/4 cup chopped fresh parsley

1. Trim the chicken of any excess fat or sinew, place in a dish and coat with the oil and garlic.
2. Peel, core and cut each apple into 8 wedges. Melt the butter in a skillet and add the apple, juice and sugar. Cook over medium heat for 25–30 minutes, turning occasionally, until caramelized.
3. Add the alcohol. Heat for 30 seconds, then, if using gas, move the pan to the side of the flame and tilt until the liquor catches. If using electricity, light with a long match. Take care and never pour liquor directly from the bottle. When the flames subside, stir in the cream.
4. Dry-fry the prosciutto until crisp, then break into large pieces. Heat a separate skillet and cook the chicken on both sides until browned and cooked through. Serve with the apple, prosciutto and parsley sprinkled over.

NUTRITION PER SERVE
Protein 35 g; Fat 30 g; Carbohydrate 25 g; Dietary Fiber 3.5 g; Cholesterol 135 mg; 520 calories

Chicken risotto

Preparation time:
  20 minutes
Total cooking time:
  40 minutes
Serves 4

5–6 cups chicken stock
1/4 cup olive oil
1/4 cup butter
2 onions, finely chopped
2 cups arborio rice
1/3 cup chopped fresh parsley
2 tablespoons chopped fresh chives
2 tablespoons chopped fresh basil
1 tablespoon chopped fresh sage
1 3/4 cups grated Parmesan
3 skinless, boned chicken breast halves
fresh chives, to garnish

1. Bring the stock to a boil in a saucepan, partially cover and reduce to a simmer.
2. Heat half the oil and butter in a separate saucepan. Cook the onion for 4 minutes until tender. Add the rice and stir for 2 minutes to coat with the oil and butter.
3. Add a ladle of stock and stir until the liquid is absorbed. Continue adding the stock a ladle at a time, stirring until it has all been absorbed and the rice is creamy and tender (this will take about 20 minutes). Stir in the herbs, half the cheese and cover.
4. Trim the chicken of any excess fat or sinew and cut into pieces. Add the remaining oil and butter to a skillet. Add the chicken in 2 batches, and cook for 5 minutes, or until golden. Season.
5. Combine the chicken with the risotto and top with the chives and the Parmesan.

NUTRITION PER SERVE
Protein 50 g; Fat 55 g; Carbohydrate 80 g; Dietary Fiber 4 g; Cholesterol 130 mg; 1045 calories

---

Normandy chicken (top) with Chicken risotto

Chicken burgers

Preparation time:
40 minutes +
2 hours marinating
Total cooking time:
20 minutes
Serves 4

$1/3$ cup extra virgin olive oil
2 cloves garlic, crushed
1 tablespoon chopped oregano
1 tablespoon chopped marjoram
1 zucchini, thinly sliced lengthwise
6 oz sweet potato, thinly sliced lengthwise
1 red sweet bell pepper, sliced into long thick slices
1 lb ground chicken
2 tablespoons mango chutney
1 onion, finely chopped
$1/2$ cup fresh bread crumbs
Middle Eastern flat bread or focaccia, to serve

1. Combine the oil, half the garlic, the oregano, marjoram, zucchini, sweet potato and red pepper in a shallow dish. Toss to combine well. Cover and marinate for 2 hours.
2. Place the chicken, mango chutney, onion, bread crumbs, remaining garlic and salt and pepper into a large bowl. Use your hands to combine the mixture well. Divide the mixture into 4 portions and shape into patties with lightly oiled hands. Place on a plate, cover with plastic wrap and refrigerate.
3. Cook the vegetables in a skillet or chargrill pan until tender, brushing with the oil while cooking.
4. Cook the burgers in the pan or grill for 5 minutes on each side, or until browned and cooked through. To serve, toast the bread and fill with the burgers and vegetables.

NUTRITION PER SERVE
Protein 30 g; Fat 25 g; Carbohydrate 20 g; Dietary Fiber 3 g; Cholesterol 60 mg; 415 calories

Chicken lasagne

Preparation time:
30 minutes
Total cooking time:
50 minutes
Serves 4

1 clove garlic, crushed
1 tablespoon oil
8 oz frozen spinach, thawed
$1/4$ cup butter
$1/4$ cup all-purpose flour
2 cups milk
1 cup shredded Cheddar
3 large sheets fresh lasagne
2 cups diced cooked or barbecued chicken
$1/2$ cup shredded Cheddar, extra

1. Preheat the oven to 350°F. Fry the garlic in the oil, then add the spinach and cook until the water has evaporated. Season and set aside.
2. Melt the butter, stir in the flour and cook for 1 minute. Add the milk gradually, stirring, then bring to a boil and cook for 2 minutes. Stir in the cheese, season and cool.
3. Add $1/2$ cup of the cheese sauce to the spinach and put $1/3$ of the spinach mixture into an ovenproof dish. Cover with a sheet of lasagne, then another $1/3$ of the spinach mixture. Sprinkle with half the chicken and cover with lasagne. Repeat with the remaining spinach, chicken and lasagne, and finish by pouring on the cheese sauce.
4. Sprinkle with the extra cheese and bake for 30–40 minutes.

NUTRITION PER SERVE
Protein 40 g; Fat 40 g; Carbohydrate 15 g; Dietary Fiber 3.5 g; Cholesterol 165 mg; 582 calories

---

Chicken burgers (top) with Chicken lasagne

❖ MARVELOUS CHICKEN RECIPES ❖

✤ **Marvelous Chicken Recipes** ✤

Finger food

These ideas for party and snack food all involve marinating chicken to add extra flavor and to keep the meat moist and tender. Marinate the chicken up to a day in advance, then just broil or bake it before serving.

Yakitori

Soak 12 bamboo skewers in water. Cut 6 skinless, boned chicken thighs into small cubes. Wipe clean 24 button mushrooms and cut 6 green onion into short lengths. Thread pieces of chicken, mushrooms and green onions onto the skewers. Mix together $1/2$ cup light soy sauce, $1/3$ cup dry sherry, 2 tablespoons soft brown sugar and 1–2 crushed cloves garlic. Pour over the skewers. Marinate for at least 1 hour. Cook the skewers on a preheated barbecue or broil for 8–10 minutes, turning and basting. Serve with soy sauce. *Makes about 12*

NUTRITION PER SERVE
Protein 11 g; Fat 2 g; Carbohydrate 2 g; Dietary Fiber 0.5 g; Cholesterol 20 mg; 75 calories

Teriyaki

Soak 12 bamboo skewers in water. Cut 1 lb skinless, boned chicken breast halves into long, thin strips. In a bowl, combine 2 tablespoons oil, $1/4$ cup light soy sauce, $1/3$ cup dry sherry, 2 tablespoons soft brown sugar, 1–2 cloves garlic and 2 teaspoons grated fresh ginger. Add the chicken, mix well, cover and refrigerate for 2 hours. Cut 1 red sweet bell pepper into cubes and 4 green onions into short lengths. Thread the chicken, red pepper and green onion alternately onto the skewers. Brush with oil and cook on a preheated barbecue or broil for 6–8 minutes, turning and basting with oil frequently. *Makes about 12*

NUTRITION PER SERVE
Protein 7.5 g; Fat 3 g; Carbohydrate 2 g; Dietary Fiber 0 g; Cholesterol 15 mg; 70 calories

❖ Finger Food ❖

Satay

Soak 16 bamboo skewers in water. Cut 1 lb skinless, boned chicken breast halves into long, thin strips. In a bowl, combine 1 tablespoon honey, $1/4$ cup soy sauce, 2 teaspoons sesame oil, 1 teaspoon each ground coriander and turmeric and $1/2$ teaspoon chili powder. Thread the chicken lengthwise onto skewers and place in the marinade. Cover and refrigerate for at least 2 hours. To make the peanut sauce, fry a small finely chopped onion in 1 tablespoon oil until soft, then stir in $1/2$ cup chunky peanut butter, 1 tablespoon soy sauce, $1/2$ cup unsweetened coconut cream and 2 tablespoons sweet chili sauce. Cook gently until heated through. Cook the skewers on a preheated barbecue or broil for 5–7 minutes, turning and basting with marinade frequently. Serve with the warm peanut sauce. *Makes about 16*

NUTRITION PER SERVE
Protein 10 g; Fat 9 g; Carbohydrate 3.5 g; Dietary Fiber 1.5 g; Cholesterol 15 mg; 135 calories

Deviled chicken wings

Combine 1 teaspoon Dijon mustard, 1 clove crushed garlic, 2 tablespoons hoisin sauce, 1 tablespoon Worcestershire sauce, 2 tablespoons tomato ketchup, 1 tablespoon lemon juice and a few drops of Tabasco in a large bowl. Season 12 chicken wings and add them to the bowl, toss together and cover with plastic wrap. Refrigerate for 2 hours or overnight. Preheat the oven to 400°F. Arrange the wings on a wire rack in a roasting pan filled with enough water to cover its base. Bake for 30–40 minutes or until the wings are browned and cooked. *Serves 4*

NUTRITION PER SERVE
Protein 8 g; Fat 4.5 g; Carbohydrate 8 g; Dietary Fiber 1.5 g; Cholesterol 25 mg; 105 calories

From left to right: Yakitori; Teriyaki; Satay; Deviled chicken wings

Index

Apricot chicken 12

Baked chicken vermicelli, 48
Burgers, chicken, 60
Buying chicken, 2

Caesar salad dressing, 4
Chicken and avocado salsa sandwich, 17
Chicken and chargrilled vegetable sandwich, 16
Chicken and herb koftas, 51
Chicken and mushroom pillows, 10
Chicken and mushroom sauté, 18
Chicken and sweet potato frittata, 56
Chicken bake, 18
Chicken burgers, 60
Chicken Caesar salad, 4
Chicken dim sums, 30
Chicken fajitas, 35
Chicken Kiev, 48
Chicken laksa, 8
Chicken lasagne, 60
Chicken liver paté, 44
Chicken noodle soup, 56
Chicken paella, 25
Chicken Parmigiana, 29
Chicken papaya salad with curry dressing, 51
Chicken pie, 12
Chicken pizza, 39
Chicken risotto, 59
Chicken schnitzels Florentine, 22
Chicken stroganoff balls, 39
Chicken terrine, 32
Chicken with salad greens and chèvre cheese, 44
Chicken, asparagus and prosciutto sandwich, 16
Chicken, prosciutto and semi-dried tomato salad, 43
Chicken, sweet pepper and feta rolls, 46–7
Chili barbecued chicken, 15
Choosing your chicken, 2–3
Coconut chicken, 8
Coq au vin, 54–5
Corn salsa, 36
Crostini with chicken livers and broiled sweet peppers, 17
Crusted chicken with corn salsa, 36
Curry dressing, 51
Curry, Thai green, 40
Cuts of chicken, 2–3

Dipping sauce for dim sums, 30
Dressings and sauces
Caesar salad, 4
curry, 51
for dim sums, 30
mustard honey, 44

Family chicken gratin, 3

Golden jeweled couscous, 52

Koftas, chicken and herb, 51

Lasagne, chicken, 60
Lemon baked chicken, 6

Macadamia-crusted chicken, 35
Mediterranean sauté, 32
Moroccan butterflied chicken, 21
Mustard honey dressing, 44

Normandy chicken, 59

Open sandwiches, 16–17

Pasta
Baked chicken vermicelli, 48
Chicken lasagne, 60
Smoked chicken and mustard linguine, 25
Vietnamese noodle salad, 40
Paté, chicken liver, 44
Pesto chicken, 29
Pie, chicken, 12
Pizza, chicken, 39

Roast chicken with garlic and potatoes, 22
Rosemary chicken fingers on bruschetta, 36

Salad
Chicken Caesar, 4
Chicken papaya, with curry dressing, 51
Chicken, prosciutto and semi-dried tomato, 43
Vietnamese noodle, 40
Salsa, corn, 36
Smoked chicken and mustard linguine, 25
Soup, chicken noodle, 56
Spicy chicken and chickpea bake, 26
Stir-fried sesame chicken and leek, 6

Tandoori chicken, 26
Tarragon chicken, 52
Thai green curry, 40

Vietnamese noodle salad, 40